PATTERNS &
PRINCIPLES

Refocusing Leadership Perspective
Developing Accuracy and Excellence

Israel Onoriobe

Table of Content

Dedication

This book is dedicated to leaders globally in the Body of Christ who are in pursuit of God, and to those whose heart are earnestly seeking to know God and to make all things according to His Patterns and Principles.

Acknowledgement

A special thanks to my editors, Tency James in Atlanta, Georgia (USA) and Mary Gray in Melbourne, Australia. You have made this book better. Thanks so much. May the Lord bless you.

My graphic designer, Pastor Favour Afimoni of Afilok Designers. Thanks for your creativity and continual support to advance the Kingdom of God through media.

Preface

Without doubt, the current state of the Church in this 21st century is comparable to the era of the children of Israel during the reign of king Ahab and Jezebel as they lost the order of God, and the people walked contrary to God.

A religious spirit has invaded the church and corrupted the hearts of many with ignorance as they can no longer discern and distinguish between good and evil, the control of a familiar spirit and the work of the Holy Spirit.

False apostles, false prophets, false pastors, false teachers and witch doctors operating with familiar spirits in the house of God are being celebrated as prophecy, prophetic powers and miracle workers, while despising authentic ministry grace and gifts the Lord has given to His Church to fulfill His purpose.

Motivational speakers and necromancers have clothed themselves with priestly garments and clergy collars; entertaining the people [and they are opposed to biblical ways, wholesome teaching and sound doctrine], thereby substituting the principles of Christ.

The distraction of the age, false glamour, the deceitfulness of riches and the passionate desire for things have choked the revelation truth of Christ in the hearts of leaders and followers alike, making them unfruitful. This greed, pride and idolatry have perverted many. The fear of God is absent from the hearts of men and there is no respect for authority as they walk in the futility of their minds. Their understanding is darkened because of a deep-seated ignorance [which is the want of knowledge and accurate perception].It is ignorance due to the blindness of hearts.

The ungodly system of this world has crept into the church unawares and many are caught by its web as it has taken root and corrupted their hearts.

Just as the children of Israel forsook God's covenant [the principles of God], tore down the altars of God [the oracle or speaking place] and killed the true prophets [the representation of the prophetic voice of God to His people].

Some of the true prophets of God were hidden in a cave by Obadiah, who was the governor of King Ahab's house, in order to preserve their lives, as they were despised by the ruling authority and the people. Their services (ministry) were cut off and replaced by the false prophets of Baalim - 1 King 18:3-4.

The leadership of King Ahab and the manipulative control and influence of Jezebel was responsible for these atrocities and abominations that caused the people to turn from God and follow after Baal (a false religious deity). Jezebel is a type of familiar spirit and principality.

'Behold, Elijah is here' - 1 King 18:8

The ministry of Elijah as a true prophet of God was a powerful instrument in that epoch that God used to redeem and restore His people.

Elijah called for the children of Israel to gather upon Mount Carmel for an open contest between him (which is a true representative of God) and the 450 prophets of Baal and the 400 prophets of grooves (the goddess of Asherah) which ate at Jezebel's table and were funded at her expense.

They were to call upon the name of their god, and he (Elijah) was to call upon the name of the LORD [Jehovah],

".....and the God who answers by fire, Him be God" - (1 King 18:20-24).

"Then Elijah said to all the people, "Come over here." So all the people came to him. He rebuilt the LORD'S altar that had been torn down. Elijah took 12 stones, one for each of the tribes named after Jacob's sons. (The LORD had spoken his word to Jacob: "Your name will be Israel."). Elijah built an altar in the LORD'S name with those stones. He also made a trench that could hold 12 quarts of grain around the altar. He arranged the wood [in order], cut up the bull, and put it on the wood. He said, "Fill four jars with water. Pour the water on the offering and on the wood." Then he said, "Do it again," and they did it again. Then he said, "Do it a third time," and they did it a third time. The water flowed around the altar, and even the trench was filled with water. When it was time to offer the sacrifice, the prophet Elijah stepped forward. He said, "LORD God of Abraham, Isaac, and Israel, make known today that you are God in Israel and that I'm your servant and have done all these things by your instructions. Answer me, LORD! Answer me! Then these people will know that you, LORD, are God and that you are winning back their hearts." So a fire from the LORD fell down and consumed the burnt offering, wood, stones, and dirt. The fire even dried up the water that was in the trench. All the people saw it and immediately bowed down to the ground. "The LORD is God!" they said. "The LORD is God!" Elijah told them, "Seize the prophets of Baal. Don't let any of them escape." The people seized them, and Elijah took them to the Kishon River and slaughtered them there" – (Kings 18:30-40 GW).

For Elijah to reveal the LORD [Jehovah] and show forth His mighty power to restore the people back to the only true God [Jehovah], he (Elijah) had to first follow by obedience the command of God's word to repair the broken altar and restore the order of the covenant of God for His people [which is the original pattern and principle God had established for them in that season of His dealing with His people]. The result was the fire of God that supernaturally fell from heaven upon the sacrifice to show to the people that the LORD [Jehovah] is the only true God.

The prophetic purpose and promise of God which is upon us *now* is the restoration of [the spirit and power of Elijah] which has a specific assignment to reconcile the body of Christ (the Church) to the Father's heart and to the wisdom of the just [which is the knowledge and holy love of the will of God] to make ready a people [perfectly] prepared for the Lord.

Another reason why the spirit and power of Elijah is needed today in the Church is for the impartation and restoration of the next generation. If we continue in the present trend of things without a genuine repentance and kingdom reformation, we are going to lose our legacy and our influence in society, and the emerging generation will be lost.

"Behold, I will send you Elijah the prophet before the coming of the great and dreadful day of the LORD: And he shall turn the heart of the fathers to the children, and the heart of the children to their fathers, lest I come and smite the earth with a curse" - (Malachi 4:5-6).

"And many of the children of Israel shall he turn to the Lord their God. And He shall go before him in the spirit and power of Elias, to turn the hearts of the fathers to the children, and the disobedient to the wisdom of the just; to make ready a people prepared for the Lord" - (Luke 1:16-17).

"The voice of him that crieth in the wilderness, Prepare ye the way of the LORD, make straight in the desert a highway for our God. Every valley shall be exalted, and every mountain and hill shall be made low: and the crooked shall be made straight, and the rough places plain: And the glory of the LORD shall be revealed, and all flesh shall see it together: for the mouth of the LORD hath spoken it" - (Isaiah 40:3-5).

The present state of the church is spiritually alarming and the bottom line is that the church needs to cry for reformation (the complete new order of setting things straight according to the patterns and principles of Christ, which God the Father has laid down for His New Testament Church).

This is only possible when a divine order is established. [A divine order is defined as the spiritual alignment of things in proper position as God has originally established them].

For a divine order to be established we must have a clear and accurate revelation and understanding of the patterns and principles of Christ and His Kingdom according to the New Covenant, and follow in total obedience to build His Church according to His will.

God is raising a people of selfless leadership whose hearts are completely turned to Him, and they are fully consumed with the pursuit of God's eternal purpose [which is Christ]. Their intense desire is to see nothing, but the formation of Christ in His people. These are the true servants (ministers) of God who have not corrupted themselves with the wine of Jezebel and the deceitfulness of this world's system. They are not title-drunk, merchants of God's grace (gifts) or hirelings who have sold their soul to the devil for fame, prosperity and power.

"Oh LORD, Restore Our Heart! Let our heart be moved by the things that move Your heart, and let our heart be broken by the things that break Your heart".

If this becomes our passion and desire, there will be a cry for reformation as we return to seek the Patterns and Principles of Christ.

Introduction

The Lord has blessed me with the grace and opportunity of traveling to several nations in every continent, covering and representing a broad spectrum of cross-cultural ministry to different people groups. For this I am eternally grateful to God our Father and the Lord Jesus Christ.

This experience of cross-cultural ministry has also given me the privilege of a cross-denominational ministry, and one of the greatest challenge I found, is NOT primarily the need for leadership, but the need for kingdom principles and an accurate biblical pattern of influence that represents Christ's purpose for the saints, and thereby, the universal Church.

The reason for saying the issue is not primarily the need for leadership is because there are several leaders in every spectrum and circle of ministry and marketplace. But the intriguing question is of the patterns and principles that govern the influence of these leaders and ministries; [if it is a true representation of the system of God's

Kingdom or a borrowed representation of Babylonian philosophy].

"The rising or the falling of our lives and the ministry will greatly depend on the kind of leadership and the principles that govern them and the priority we give to reproduce accurate leadership after God's eternal purpose and the principles of His Kingdom".

This is what has compelled me to write this book and pen down some important biblical principles to give us some insight and understanding regarding; The Purpose of Leadership, The Importance of Leadership, The Impact [Blessing] of Leadership, The Lost Leadership and The Effect of Leadership.

As we journey through these thoughts, my prayer is that we will discover and understand accurately the Patterns and Principles of Christ that govern His Kingdom, so we can allow a change or paradigm shift where necessary. I pray that the process of transformation to bring a true Kingdom of God influence and a significant impartation upon our lives and ministry will also be clear.

Imagine when the fullness of God's glory is revealed in the Church, and the influence and impact of that upon the earth. What we are seeing today is a measure that is less than normal. The power and the glory of God that was promised by God is yet to be fully manifested upon the Church. The fullness is possible only; when things are set in divine order as God has ordained; the Sons of God are rightly positioned in their place, knowing who and Whose they are; when the fear of God [His holy reverence] becomes the core value of our heart as we walk in total obedience following the patterns and principles of Christ. These are some of the fundamentals for the glory of God to be revealed.

Chapter One

Christ - The Measurement of Grace given

In March 2017, while on an apostolic mission in Brazil, the Lord began to impress strongly on my heart during my time of devotion in the early hours of the morning about the significance and need to understand and recognize the measure of grace which He has given to us [His Church]. The Lord was saying to me that there is a need for us to understand accurately and receive the full gifts of the five-fold ministry according to Ephesians 4:7-16, if we are to mature {grow spiritually} and fulfill His purpose on earth as His Church.

Initially I was resisting the need to share this message with the churches in Brazil at that time because my Portuguese translator was rather inexperienced, making it very difficult for me to communicate effectively and I did not want to start a message that I could not fully explain or finish.

Secondly as I traveled on that trip within the nation of Brazil, I could see the spiritual immaturity among the saints as I was trying to measure their level of maturity, concerned they were not ready for this teaching. But the Lord ministered to my heart reminding me that these were His people and He determines their growth, and above all He gives revelation and understanding; *not me.*

The highlight of the message, as the Lord was ministering to me, was that the reason why the body of Christ lacks spiritual growth, development and maturity, as well as the distress of the Church and her ineffectiveness in fulfilling her purpose on earth, is because of the gross level of spiritual ignorance and the lost priority in understanding the true purpose of the five-fold ministry and modeling an accurate pattern for ministry [servant leadership].

There is an adverse effect in our lives, in the Church and ultimately in society when the true purpose of ministry [servant leadership] is lost. Everything is shaped by leadership. The moral decline in the Church and the society is a result of the lack of true servant leadership that represents the divine purpose of God.

"But unto every one of us is given grace according to the measure of the gift of Christ. Wherefore He saith, When He ascended up on high, He led captivity captive, and gave gifts unto men.......And He gave some, apostles; and some, prophets; and some, evangelists; and some, pastors and teachers" – Ephesians 4:7-8, 11.

It is important to note exactly what Paul the apostle was saying; "the grace that was given to us {the church} as a gift, is Christ Himself, which is the measurement of Himself that He measured as gifts and distributed into five personalities which are now called apostles, prophets, evangelists, pastors and teachers.

The sum of this GRACE is Christ Himself.

Christ is the Apostle.
Christ is the Prophet.
Christ is the Evangelist.
Christ is the Shepherd (Pastor).
Christ is the Teacher.

Each of these gifts is a measure of the grace of God, which is Christ Himself, wrapped in a human vessel and given to dispense to the saints. These human vessels are grace carriers that impart a dimension of Christ to the Church.

The combination of all five ministry gifts imparted to the body of Christ is the formation of grace that produces Christ in us, and brings us into the fullness of the stature of Christ Himself [which is the desire the Father purposed for His Church before the foundation of the world; so, we become like His Son, Christ].

"For whom He did foreknow, He also did predestinate *to be* conformed to the image of His Son - [He had decided to let them become like His Own Son], that He might be the firstborn among many brethren" – Romans 8:29.

Every saint has received a gift from God to serve a specific purpose for the kingdom of God according to 1 Peter 4:10, but it is imperative that we also know that some [*not all*] are the very gift themselves, wrapped in human vessels and given from God for ministry to the saints according to Ephesians 4:7-13.

For those whom Christ has called into the five-fold ministry, they must find their true purpose and primary assignment in Him, and function in the measure of His grace given to them in fulfillment of His purpose.

"Is not this the Carpenter, the son of Mary and the brother of James and Joses and Judas and Simon? And are not His sisters here among us? And they took offense at Him and were hurt [that is, they disapproved of Him, and it hindered them from acknowledging His authority] and they were caused to stumble and fall. But Jesus said to them, A prophet is not without honor (deference, reverence) except in his [own] country and among [his] relatives and in his [own] house. And He was not able to do even one work of power there, except that He laid His hands on a few sickly people [and] cured them. And He marveled because of their unbelief (their lack of faith in Him). And He went about among the surrounding villages and continued teaching" - Mark 6:3-6 AMPC.

Unbelief in the grace of God upon a man will bring offense and disapproval of God's authority in him; and when the grace of God is not acknowledged it causes us to stumble and fall.

I pray that we would fully understand and receive the gifts the Lord Jesus Christ has given to us as His Church, so we will not stumble and fall, but walk in the fulness of His will and purpose for us.

Chapter Two

Principal Objectives of the Five-Fold Ministries

Every five-fold ministry grace that is operating accurately according to the pattern and principles of Christ will make these following objectives their primary goal, and they will function with an authentic apostolic spirit that fulfills them in the body of Christ.

It is imperative to understand that according to Ephesians 4:11-16, the ultimate purpose for the five-fold ministry is to produce the following fruits in the saints and corporately in the universal Church by:

1. Perfecting and equipping the saints so they should do the work of the ministry toward building up and edifying the Church, which is Christ's body — Verse 12.

2. Developing the body of Christ until we all come to the unity of the faith — Verse 13.

3. Bringing the saints to the full and accurate knowledge of Christ, who is the Son of God — Verse 13.

4. Bringing the saints to a "Perfect Man" - Growing spiritually to a completeness of personality, which is nothing less than the standard height of Christ's own perfection – Verse 13.

5. Bringing the saints to the measure of the completeness and of the fullness of Christ – Verse 13.

6. Stimulating the Church to love - speaking the truth in love and building itself up in love. Love is the underlying basis of the Church's function and it is the reflection of Christ's nature – Verse 15 & 16.

7. Building the body to be closely joined and firmly knit together so that each part is working properly in all its function, causing a corporate activation of the saints to work effectively as ONE BODY in fulfilling its purpose – Verse 16.

Every ministry gift must give priority and focus to fulfill this purpose. When this is fully accomplished, it means that the Church has attained the full stature of spiritual maturity, which is Christ Himself, but until then the five-fold ministry gifts (grace) will continue to function in the body of Christ.

Remember, the full measure and stature of maturity is CHRIST. We can only attain to this height through the comprehension of the FULL and ACCURATE knowledge of the Son of God.

"The growth and development of people is the highest calling of leadership" - Harvey S. Firestone.

If the ministry is not prioritizing to produce these fruits and fulfilling the ultimate purpose of God in fully equipping and perfecting the saints to the complete stature of the fulness of Christ, then something is wrong with the patterns and principles being applied and imparted to the saints through our teaching and preaching.

That is why the effective functioning of the office and ministry of the five-fold gifts is needed in the Church today.

There is an urgent necessity for true Kingdom apostolic leaders and ministries according to Ephesians 4:11-16, to rise and travail for Christ to be formed again in His Church. This is a clarion call for the reintroduction of CHRIST to His Church so that we might know Him and grow into His fullness.

Chapter Three

Developing Excellence in Life & Ministry

God is a God of Patterns and Principles.

It is very important for us to understand New Testament patterns and principles that reflect the true nature and character of Christ in our lives and in His Church. Those who will not recognize and follow the patterns of God will soon realize that they have degenerated into irrelevance and become an abomination {a thing that causes disgust or loathing} in the sight of God.

"All this, said David, the LORD made me understand in writing by His hand upon me, even all the works of this pattern" - 1 Chronicles 28:19.

The whole pattern - [the construction plan] for all the building of the house, David said, the LORD has shown and made clear to him so he could build accurately according to that order.

"They serve as a pattern and foreshadowing of [what has its true existence and reality in] the heavenly things (sanctuary). For when Moses was about to erect the tabernacle, he was warned by God, saying, "See that you make it all [exactly] according to the pattern which was shown to you on the mountain." - Hebrews 8:5 Amplified Bible.

"According to all that I shew thee, after the pattern of the tabernacle and the pattern of all the instruments thereof, even so shall ye make it........And look that thou make them after their pattern, which was shewed thee in the mount" - Exodus   25:9,   40.

Moses was divinely instructed and cautioned to do everything according to the pattern given by God. This pattern reflected the true existence and reality of things in heaven   being   done   on   earth.

A pattern is an original design or system that is repeated or discernible in the order in which something happens or is done.

[Patterns & Principles are examples of spiritual instructions and divine plans the Lord has given and shown to us in the scriptures for us to follow for the fulfilment of His divine purpose and Kingdom. Failure to do this will result in a shipwreck of our faith and the ultimate failure of our works].

Life and Ministry has a divine pattern that God has set as an order for things to be done by us, and these patterns are the fundamental truth or principle that serves as the foundation of the system of God's Kingdom, or the functioning of authentic apostolic and prophetic ministries and Kingdom oriented people.

You can have a brilliant ministry profile and mission statement, and yet be of no relevance to the purposes of God on earth, except the patterns and principles of Christ are followed in all their particularity and completeness.

The development of excellence in life and ministry will require that we know, and follow the patterns and principles of Christ and His Kingdom [which He has laid out and revealed to us]. There is a need for accurate prophetic understanding of God's purpose to manifest His excellence, because anything less than this will not produce or fulfill God's original purpose for our lives and ministry.

The life of Jesus Christ is the pattern or spiritual model which is revealed and given in scripture as an example for us believers to follow to become like Him. The lack of Christ's pattern and principle in our lives and in the body of Christ will result to the lack of divine order.

"Brethren, join in following my example, and note those who so walk, as you have us for a pattern. For many walk, of whom I have told you often, and now tell you even weeping, that they are the enemies of the cross of Christ: whose end is destruction, whose god is their belly, and whose glory is in their shame—who set their mind on earthly things. For our citizenship is in heaven, from which we also eagerly wait for the Savior, the Lord Jesus Christ" - Philippians 3:17-20 NKJV.

It is important to note from the above scripture: verse 17, and from the full context of that chapter, that Paul did not say he nor the apostles are THE Pattern to be followed, but he admonished the Philippians to join and follow them as one who is in pursuit to reach the goal of the prize of the upward call of God in Christ, who is THE Pattern.

Christ is the ONLY standard of pattern and principle for the New Testament saints/Church.

As members of God's household, we must be conscious of the fact that we are *not* of this world [with its systems], but we are of God and His Kingdom and our citizenship is in heaven.

"Consequently, you are no longer foreigners and strangers, but fellow citizens with God's people (the saints) and also members of His (God's) household" - Ephesians 2:19.

This implies that we must be governed by the system of the Kingdom of God with its rules and principles, and not set our mind on earthly things [which are the temporal systems of this world].These earthly systems are in opposition to the patterns and principles of Christ and make us to become enemies of the cross, bringing destruction to us.

There is a "Kingdom System" for all things!

A system can be defined as a set of laws by which things function. Without the law, there is no order. Therefore

"Kingdom Systems" are "laws" or "principles" that govern the functioning of God's Kingdom to bring order.

Kingdom Systems are not natural laws, but spiritual laws. God's will and purpose cannot be fulfilled by the operation of natural laws, but only by the application of spiritual laws and principles.

There are different patterns and principles which are carnal laws and worldly standards of measurement by which ungodly men conduct and pattern themselves for success.

We as the body of Christ should not sit down and figure things out by our own carnal imaginations, or copy things from the perspective of the world's standard and apply them as principles, and making them the spiritual standard for the functioning of our lives and ministries, simply because we want to be successful or be counted among the elite.

True success in God's Kingdom can only be measured by the application of God's patterns and principles, and the fulfillment of His original purpose for our lives and ministry in everything we do.

To be governed, every nation or kingdom has a constitution with fundamental principles that are acknowledged. Likewise, the Bible containing the Holy Scriptures, is the only constitution (fundamental principles) of heaven and the Kingdom of God, and is the spiritual authority by which God governs His people (the saints).

A kingdom principle is a spiritual truth, method, or rule adopted as the basis for action or conduct [which is taught in scripture] and it becomes a fundamental truth that serves as a foundation for a system of belief.

"Your Kingdom come, Your will be done, on earth as it is in heaven" – Matthew 6:10 ESV.

Every true believer of Christ must desire the will of God to be reflected on earth as it is in heaven.

Kingdom systems {Patterns and Principles} that are established by the Church must be the will of God and a reflection of the true existence and reality of things in heaven being done here on earth.

Measuring the Pattern

Prophet Ezekiel was a protagonist, who advocated for a reformation with much of his ministry centered on issues concerning the restoration of the temple of God that was in ruins. His call was for the return of Israel back to the old pathway the Lord had laid out for His people and for the proper alignment of things for the glory of God to be restored.

Prophet Ezekiel stressed the importance of the restoration of the true patterns and principles for God's temple for the flow of God's power and glory to be manifested among the people.

As covenant believers, we must understand that the true house of God is the house that is built by Jesus Christ, [which is built according to His pattern and principle]. Whatever is built by men with external regulations will not meet God's approval and His glory will not manifest.

There are specific patterns and principles the Lord has set for His people, which are fundamental for our moral conduct and worship, but the children of Israel went to set up their own patterns and built a wall of separation between them and God, resulting in their worship being rejected by God.

God said, they have "*set up their thresholds by my thresholds*" and "*their posts by my posts*". This means they have built and established their own patterns and principles.

"And He [the Lord] said to me, "Son of man, this is the place of My throne and the place of the soles of My feet, where I will dwell in the midst of the sons (descendants) of Israel forever. And the house of Israel will not again defile My holy name, neither they nor their kings, by their [idolatrous] prostitution and by the corpses and monuments of their kings in their graves, by setting their threshold by My threshold and their doorpost beside My doorpost, with [only] the wall between Me and them. They have defiled and desecrated My holy name by the vile atrocities which they have committed. So I have consumed them in My anger. Now let them put far away from Me their [idolatrous] prostitution and the corpses and monuments of their kings, and I will dwell in their midst forever" - Ezekiel 43:7-9 Amplified Bible.

Because of this God told Ezekiel to "*show the house to the house*". In other words, he was asked to reveal the original pattern of God's house to the people, so they could look at God's pattern and measure the pattern in comparison to the house they built, if it is according to His pattern or if they have established their own pattern.

"Thou son of man, shew the house to the house of Israel, that they may be ashamed of their iniquities; and let them measure the pattern" - Ezekiel 43:10.

When we teach the traditions and commandments of men, which are contrary to Biblical doctrine and set up our own patterns of operation, our own denomination, our own religious rules and our own method of church growth principles, we are setting up a false standard of measurement.

We are often concerned with our external form and regulations but neglect the internal process of the heart. The outward fashion and glamour is temporal, but God weighs the intent of the heart. He is more concerned with our conscience and the character of our heart because that is the place of His eternal measurement for the motive of what we do, if it is in line with His will, or if it is from the selfish motive of our soul-realm?

Unfortunately, some of the things we have been consumed with, which we have called the vision of God and the leading of the Holy Spirit, have been our own selfish ambition which has driven us, thus void of God's Spirit and will.

Many have displaced the original vision and purpose of God's house with their own personal and selfish ambition and they are building the saints inaccurately in falsehood - [unsound doctrine and false messages].

We need to constantly check the motive of our hearts on the scale of God's word so we can be tried and proven in all things that we do as true and wise master-builders, so that the heavenly pattern is established on earth.

"Examine me, O Lord, and prove me; Try my mind and my heart" - Psalm 26:2 NKJV.

This will position our hearts and allow us to understand divine knowledge, so our mind and thoughts will realign to the mind of Christ, to walk circumspectly, and build according to divine order - precepts upon precepts, lines upon lines.

Following the Patterns and Principles of Christ is the pathway to receiving the life of God and to giving honour to Him.

God desires honour that comes from the heart reflecting the place He has in our heart. We glorify God when we accurately reflect the character of Christ through His patterns and principles as we observe to do according to His will. To glorify God is to honour God! Beyond our lip service we must demonstrate our honour for God through our works and actions (Isaiah 29:13).

Chapter Four

Developing Accurate Perception

One of the greatest hindrances to the understanding and development of Kingdom patterns and principles affecting our excellence in life and ministry is our "mindset", because, *you cannot grow beyond your thinking.* You are a product of your thought!

The greater part of our Christian walk is the realignment of our thoughts to the will of Christ and His Kingdom, because accurate thinking will produce accurate lifestyle and leadership.

Wrong thinking affects the effectiveness of true kingdom leadership and the principles of Godly living. Inaccurate perception opposes Christological pattern and principles and this ultimately hinders the development of excellence in our lives and ministry.

A clear example of this can be seen between the Pharisees and Jesus Christ in Mark 7:1-13. Their traditional thinking, which was carnally rooted in their philosophy and ideology, was a great hindrance and opposition against the patterns and principles of Jesus Christ.

Jesus said to them:

"You disregard and give up and ask to depart from you the commandment of God and cling to the tradition of men [keeping it carefully and faithfully]. And He said to them, You have a fine way of rejecting [thus thwarting and nullifying and doing away with] the commandment of God in order to keep your tradition [your own human regulations and ways of doing things]" - Mark 7:8-9 Amplified Bible.

Thus, you are "making the word of God of no effect through your tradition which you have handed down. And many such things you do" - Mark 7:13 NKJV.

Your perception of God and His purpose will both make room for you and enthrone you to a place of destiny and the ultimate fulfillment of divine purpose or it will limit your potential and rob you of divine opportunities and ultimately your purpose and destiny in life.

"And she said unto her husband, Behold now, I perceive that this is an holy man of God, which passeth by us continually. Let us make a little chamber, I pray thee, on the wall; and let us set for him there a bed, and a table, and a stool, and a candlestick: and it shall be, when he cometh to us that he shall turn in thither" - 2 Kings 4:9-10.

Her perception of the character and totality of a holy God upon Elisha caused her to make a room for the grace of God which resulted to the birth of her miracle child - 2 Kings 4:14-17.

"And David perceived that the LORD had confirmed him king over Israel, for his kingdom was lifted up on high, because of his people Israel" - 1 Chronicles 14:2.

The fulfillment of David's enthronement was because of his perception of God's confirmation. You will be enthroned and established, or you will be dethroned and destabilized by your perception. Your perception is your reality.

Your perception of things will always determine your reaction. For this reason, we must be sensitive at all times to the leading of the Holy Spirit to comprehend fully the patterns and principles of God, especially when we are favoured with divine moments of revelation and heavenly encounters.

The Holy Spirit is the key access for developing accurate perception and revelation.

"The David gave Solomon his son the plans.... And the plans of all that he had by the Spirit, of the courts of the house of the Lord...." – 1 Chronicles 28:11-12.

To establish accurate patterns and principles for the fulfillment of God's purpose in all things we must allow the Holy Spirit to outwork the will of God in us and through us without any external regulations. This is how we can fully align with God's will and agenda and see an accurate manifestation of His patterns and principles.

The totality of our consummation in all things must become the manifestation of His will. Our will, emotions, intellect and desire must be the will of God in all things.

The Church must function with apostolic and prophetic precision. This is where the true ministry grace of the apostles and prophets must be seen at work as a more excellent ministry, revealing and establishing the patterns and principles of God which are fundamental to the Church. In this way we can know the will of God and become the instrument of its fulfillment. Not false apostles and false prophets parading ourselves as magicians, entertainers and celebrities and making a mockery and public shame of God's house and His people.

Everything from salvation is based on revelation. What we become and the fulfillment of our life's purpose will be by revelation. Therefore, Paul the apostle prayed earnestly for the church in Ephesus when he heard of their faith in the Lord Jesus and their love for all the saints:

"That the God of our Lord Jesus Christ, the Father of glory, may give unto you the spirit of wisdom and revelation in the knowledge of Him: The eyes of your understanding being enlightened; that ye may know what is the hope of His calling, and what the riches of the glory of His inheritance in the saints" - Ephesians 1:17-18.

Our perspective must be elevated to an upward view and be wrapped with the heavenly order. We must see the blue print and build by the original plan. Just like Jesus the pattern-Son said, "*The Son can do nothing of Himself, but what He seeth the Father do: for what things soever He doeth, these also doeth the Son likewise*" - John 5:19. This is the only way to go so that our lives and works would become pleasing and acceptable to God.

Heaven is transmitting and downloading the mindset of Christ for His Kingdom, but the question is, are we connected? Are we plugged in? When God speaks and reveals His patterns we must act and make it a reality. Heaven's design must be our blueprint in all things – [on earth as it is in heaven].

The abundant life of God comes through the accurate knowledge of God that is imparted into our spirit man, resurrecting and awakening the reality of the Spirit of life in us.

Until we have a clear and accurate understanding (revelation) of the Lord and His purposes, our professed faith and works will become a mere religion that is worthless. The full life and power of God lays in our comprehension of the full and accurate knowledge of Jesus Christ, who is the pattern-Son of God.

I pray that your life will be a true expression of God's will on earth.

Chapter Five

Refocusing Leadership Perspective

Have you ever sincerely asked yourself the true meaning and purpose of leadership and ministry, according to Christ's perspective for His kingdom?

Many of today's emerging leaders and churches have defined spiritual leadership and ministry through methods that are influenced by multiple factors based on the modern systems of this world. These systems have become their standard of measurement. Without doubt the principal role and the eternal purpose of God for kingdom leadership and ministry will be lost until there is a clear revelation and understanding of God's intent for this, hence, there is a need to have a 'Refocused Leadership Perspective' to rediscover the pattern and principle of Christ.

"Ministry" comes from the Greek word "diakonia", which means "to serve or to be a servant" - it also has a root word "douleuo", meaning "to serve as a bond slave". In the New Testament, the concept of ministry was service to God and to people in the name of Jesus.

I have researched for the word "leader(s)" or "leadership" in the New Testament bible in context to Jesus Christ and the early apostles' teaching of leadership, and it would interest you to know that in the New Testament there is no record of Jesus Christ teaching His disciples the doctrine of leadership in line with what is popularly taught and perceived today in churches as the concept of leadership.

Jesus only taught His disciples servanthood. In the Bible what we call 'leadership' today is known as 'servanthood', and the word 'ministry' meant service as in the office of a servant.

Jesus didn't call twelve LEADERS, He called twelve SERVANTS known as the disciples or the apostles of the Lord Jesus Christ. He didn't call them to LEAD, He called them to SERVE.

The basic concept of the pattern and principle of Jesus' ministry was servanthood. This is one of the patterns and principles missing today in most ministries, leadership styles and method; and this missing concept is disqualifying our work before the Lord.

The twelve disciples known as the apostles, once had a dispute among themselves on the road, after Jesus informed them about His coming betrayal and death (Mark 9:30-32). They did not understand what He was saying, and they were afraid to ask Him what He meant, instead they discussed and argued about '*who should be the greatest*'; that is to say, 'who should be the leader?', but Jesus called them and taught them the correct pathway:

"What was it that ye disputed among yourselves by the way? But they held their peace: for by the way they had disputed among themselves, who should be the greatest. And He sat down, and called the twelve, and saith unto them, If any man desire to be first, the same shall be last of all, and servant of all" - Mark 9:33-35.

Again, two brothers, James and John, who were part of the twelve, made a request and asked Jesus to make them chief on the Council of the Twelve Apostles! One asked to sit on the right-hand of Christ when He sat on His 'glorious throne', and the other asked to be seated on His left-hand. This request from James and John greatly displeased the other ten apostles, but Jesus called them to Him and made a profound revelation to them concerning His principle by which they must abide as His disciples:

"Jesus called His disciples and told them, "You know that those who are recognized as rulers {leaders, chief} among the gentiles lord it over them {holding them in subjection}, and their superiors act like tyrants {exercising authority and dominion} over them. That's not the way it should be among you. Instead, whoever wants to become great among you must be your servant and whoever wants to be first among you must be a slave to everyone, because even the Son of Man did not come to be served, but to serve and to give His life as a ransom for many people" - Mark 10:42-45 ISV {Emphasis is mine}.

Clearly Jesus was explaining that those who belong to this world's system have called themselves leaders to lord over the people, but; "...*it shall not be so among you*" - Mark 10:43. Jesus provided for us the pattern for ministry - "He came, *not to receive service, but to give it and serve*" - Mark 10:45.

To be a true servant of Christ, this is the way it should be among us who belong to the Kingdom of God and who operate by God's system.

True kingdom ministers and ministries must understand that they are divinely called to be SERVANTS of God, servants of the Lord Jesus Christ and servants to His Church. We are called to SERVE the Body of Christ.

If we cannot SERVE then we cannot LEAD. The spiritual principle of authentic kingdom ministry and Christ's leadership is service. It is bearing the office of a servant.

The five-fold ministry is composed of the five gifts of grace - apostles, prophets, evangelists, pastors (shepherds of His flock) and teachers, and they are given to the Church by the Lord Jesus Christ.

These gifts of grace are a divine calling to the service of servant-hood and NOT an office to lord or wield authority over the saints, who are joint-heirs and inheritance of Christ.

If we clearly understand the saying of Jesus in Mark 9:35 and Mark 10:45, we would understand without doubt that the original intent of the five-fold ministry is not a calling for anyone to be "first in ranking" or to be chief, head, boss or number one in office, but rather it is a calling to be the last and the servant of all.

Even Paul the apostle made this bold statement, which is often undermined, that; "God has placed us apostles last in line, like people condemned to die. We have become a spectacle for people and angels to look at" - 1 Corinthians 4:9 GW.

We are so fond of highlighting the Greek word "proton", meaning "first", taken from 1 Corinthians 12:28, and emphasizing the fact that 'God has appointed the apostles to be first. The wrong perception which many have embraced from this is to think that the apostles have been divinely elevated by God to be a superior position, and to be more important than others, or to be chief among others. This has endeared many to desire the office and title of an 'apostle' to make them feel important, which has resulted to every Jack and Harry in the church today calling themselves apostles. Even some who carry a spirit of Jezebel are calling themselves apostles.

The proper meaning of the Greek word "proton" - "to be first" as applied in context to the apostles in the scriptures, is to be; "first in the order of service" [being a servant] and in function as a foundational ministry, laying the foundation for the building of the house of God [and the foundation is Christ].

In the building of a house, those who lay the foundation are the 'first to labour' before the others build upon that which is laid. This doesn't make those who lay the foundation more important than the other labourers, but by job description they are simply first to labour. This is the same principle that applies to the apostles being appointed by God as "first" in the Church to serve. They are pioneers of divine service.

"Having been built on the foundation of the apostles and prophets, with Christ Jesus Himself as the [chief] Cornerstone, in whom the whole structure is joined together, and it continues [to increase] growing into a holy temple in the Lord [a sanctuary dedicated, set apart, and sacred to the presence of the Lord]. In Him [and in fellowship with one another] you also are being built together into a dwelling place of God in the Spirit" - Ephesians 2:20-23 Amplified Bible.

"According to the grace of God which is given unto me, as a wise master builder, I [Paul an apostle] have laid the foundation [which is Christ], and another [other ministry grace] buildeth thereon. But let every man take heed how he buildeth thereupon" - 1 Corinthians 3:10 (Emphasis is mine).

If there is anyone to be "first", it is simply the one who goes ahead of others to lead by example through his service of being a servant, so others are motivated to follow the Christ in him for the fulfillment of His will and purpose.

The apostles in scripture did not address themselves as "leaders" nor did they claim to be in "leadership", rather, they considered themselves to be 'bond servants of Christ' sent to serve the Church. They were simply following the teaching and example of Jesus, Who is THE Pattern.

Paul the apostle addressed himself as a bond servant of Jesus Christ:

"Paul, a bondservant of Jesus Christ, called to be an apostle, separated to the gospel of God" - Romans 1:1 NKJV.

"Paul, a servant of God, and an apostle of Jesus Christ, according to the faith of God's elect, and the acknowledging of the truth which is after godliness" - Titus 1:1.

"For though I be free from all men, yet have I made myself servant unto all, that I might gain the more" - 1 Corinthians 9:19.

Peter addressed himself as a servant and an apostle of Jesus Christ:

"Simon Peter, a servant and an apostle of Jesus Christ, to them that have obtained like precious faith with us through the righteousness of God and our Saviour Jesus Christ" - 2 Peter 1:1.

James identified himself as a servant of God and of the Lord Jesus Christ:
"James, a servant of God and of the Lord Jesus Christ, to the twelve tribes which are scattered abroad, greeting" - James 1:1.

The greatest honour of ministry is servanthood. Just like the parable of the talents, at the end when the Lord shall make reckoning of all things, it shall be said, "*Well done, good and faithful servant*" - Matthew 25:21, not "Well done, good and faithful leader, master, bishop, chief apostle or major prophet etc". More so, at the consummation of all things; "*before the throne of God and of the Lamb shall be His servants serving Him, and they shall see His face, and His name shall be on their foreheads*" - Revelation 22:3-4.

Therefore, the pathway to become a ruler in God's Kingdom at the consummation of all things is to be a faithful servant.

"This is how one should regard us [the apostles], as servants of Christ and stewards of the mysteries of God" - 1 Corinthians 4:1 - English Standard Version.

The highest form and the greatest honour and fulfillment of leadership in the Kingdom of God is service {being a servant}, because this is the purpose!

"He who is greatest among you shall be your servant" – Matthew 23:11.

A servant is one who has no will. His absolute desire is to please his master by doing the master's will. The desire of the master is his desire. As disciples and servants of God and the Lord Jesus Christ, this must be the attitude and desire of our heart in order to fulfill God's will in our lives and ministry.

"For who is the greater, the one who reclines at table (the master), or the one who serves? Is it not the one who reclines at table? But I am in your midst as One Who serves" – Luke 22:27 Amplified Bible.

"When we, as followers of Jesus, finally realize that our calling is to serve - not merely to seek our own interests - then we will have an irresistible impact on our clients, our colleagues, and our community" - Dr. Walt Larimore.

"If you and I are to make the impact in life upon others that we should; if we are to fulfill God's purpose and plan for our life; and if we're to reap the maximum blessings that God has prepared for us; we, too, must develop the spirit of a servant, and our actions must be the actions of a servant. A servant who realizes that Jesus is not only our Savior, but He is the Master of our life. Any unwillingness

or resistance to serve others in His name is an act of rebellion" - Dr. Charles Stanley.

When we lose focus on this primary principle of life and ministry, which is service, it will result in the inevitable consequence of our true value and purpose being lost.

Ministry is principle and *not* position. Our significance and the development of excellence in life and ministry comes from living by principle, *and not by position*. Those who value position more than principle will soon lose both.

Efficiency and excellence in life and ministry requires that we adhere to the principles of Christ and His Kingdom, and by this we can significantly influence people and make an impact in our world.

"The key to successful leadership today is influence, not authority" - Ken Blanchard.

Religion offers people position in life and ministry, but the Kingdom of God offers people principles. Redemption is not primarily about a restoration to position or place of dominion, but it is a restoration of principle and purpose. <u>The goal of man's dominion is to SERVE God's purpose.</u>

The plan of God from the beginning was for man and woman to be fruitful, multiply, replenish and subdue the earth. God's purpose for them was to rule, having complete authority and dominion over the creation order. They were to govern creation and keep the earth under the rule of God as it is in heaven. They were blessed (empowered) to fulfill this purpose. This means their government was to SERVE God's purpose. They were blessed to serve, so are we blessed to serve!

"God said, Let Us [Father, Son, and Holy Spirit] make mankind in Our image, after Our likeness, and let them have complete authority over the fish of the sea, the birds of the air, the [tame] beasts, and over all of the earth, and over everything that creeps upon the earth. So God created man in His own image, in the image and likeness of God He created him; male and female He created them. And God blessed them and said to them, Be fruitful, multiply, and fill the earth, and subdue it [using all its vast resources in the service of God and man]; and have dominion over the fish of the sea, the birds of the air, and over every living creature that moves upon the earth" - Genesis 1:26-28 Amplified Bible.

God's blessing is connected to His purpose in and for us; and it is to serve. The blessing of God is a blessing of purpose. God only blesses purpose. We must therefore understand the purpose of God for us and His original plan for our salvation, so we can serve creation to fulfill God's will on earth. This is how we receive and walk in the blessings of God.

Unfortunately, we desire and fight for power, prestige, high positions and impressive titles to make us feel valuable, acceptable or of great significance. This misplaced priority and quest for titles, positions, dominion, status and power has opened the doors for sorcerers and familiar spirits to penetrate within the circle of believers to rule and control many. As the body of Christ we must get rid of this 'celebrity spirit' that is tied to the worldly concept of leadership and which is corrupting the minds of people and robbing the Church of her true purpose and glory of service.

This is one of the biggest challenges we have among leaders. We begin well in our high calling in God, but end up turning things around and making an idol of ourselves by building towards our own ambitions, establishing our own pet-names, 'my ministry', 'my church' and 'my kingdom', rather than the name of the Lord Jesus Christ and His Kingdom.

We should not compromise the principles of the Kingdom of God and deny the patterns of Christ because of our desire for worldly positions and the applause of men. Rather, we should surround ourselves with genuine men and women of kingdom principles whose life and ministry are governed by the rule of heaven, instead of being bound by the positions of men [or as men of positions] and miss the mark of His calling upon us to serve. Selah!

Chapter Six

God's Pattern for Leadership & Ministry

Leadership is Servanthood!

The spirit of true leadership is servanthood. Spiritual leadership is a call to servanthood {service}, *not masterhood*. We have too many masters, but few servants.

Jesus taught and modeled a different order of spiritual calling in totality. Regardless of His divinity and His popularity, Christ Jesus remained committed to His service as a servant. This nature of Christ must be seen in and through us in our words, in our actions and in our attitude.

As we look into the account of John 13:1-17, there is so much to be learnt as we follow the leadership principle of Jesus as our ultimate standard and pattern.

"[Now] before the Passover Feast began, Jesus knew (was fully aware) that the time had come for Him to leave this world and return to the Father. And as He had loved those who were His own in the world, He loved them to the last and to the highest degree. So [it was] during supper, Satan having already put the thought of betraying Jesus in the heart of Judas Iscariot, Simon's son, [That] Jesus, knowing (fully aware) that the Father had put everything into His hands, and that He had come from God and was [now] returning to God. Got up from supper, took off His garments, and taking a [servant's] towel, He fastened it around His waist" – John 13:1-4 Amplified Bible.

Jesus knew who He was; He possessed the fullness of the attributes which make God God. There was no question of His identity in God. He was fully aware of His position with the Father, [as The Son of God], that He had come from God and was going to God. With this assurance in Him, '*He humbled Himself and took off His garments and laid it aside*' and took a servant's towel and wrapped it around His waist. After that, He poured water into a basin and bent down and began to wash His disciples' feet.

His position of being essentially one with God and in the form of God, did not compromise His responsibility to serve His disciples, rather, He striped Himself of all privileges and rightful dignity, to assume the form of a servant (slave). He did this as He took off His garment and laid it aside. Through the arc of scripture, a garment is a picture of identity, honour, authority, beauty, royalty, dignity and righteousness. His garment also speaks of His glory, yet He laid it aside and took the place and likeness of a servant to serve.

When we truly discover and know who we are in Christ, serving others will not be intimidating or become a threat to us and to our ministry, because it doesn't compromise our calling and who we are as Sons of God. As we can see, after washing the disciples' feet, which are the lowest part of man, Christ took and put on His garment, which He had laid aside and sat down again, signifying the taking up of His position;

"After Jesus had washed His disciples' feet and had put His outer garment back on, He sat down again. Then He said: Do you understand what I have done?" – John 13:12 CEV.

As a Teacher (Master), His posture of taking the form of a servant and a servant's towel and His service of ministering to His disciples' feet did not rob Him of His identity and position as God. *He could put on His garment again and then sit down and continue to be Who He was and do what He was assigned by the Father to do.*

So many people want ministry but they don't want to serve. They love the portfolio of ministry without the responsibility of service because they think service [being a servant to the people] will rob them of their dignity and identity. Many people view servanthood as a sign of weakness and dishonor, yet, from Jesus' perspective, it was a position of strength and honor. It takes more strength of character to serve than to be served, and this was the example that Jesus demonstrated as He washed His disciple's feet to set a standard for them to follow as His disciples (apostles). He didn't seek for honor, He extended it. He didn't long for respect, He gave it to them. What an epitome of humility and servanthood!

The true ministry of Christ is service to humanity. Any ministry that is void of this responsibility is only a worthless religion.

When we know who we are and Who's we are, being assured of our relationship in and with Christ with our true purpose and calling in Him, carnal desire, seeking for self-relevance and fighting for one's own honor will die. Because we do not seek for honor and acceptance through leadership and ministry, rather, we function in His service, from His honour and His acceptance, which the Father has already given to us as His beloved sons.

We are the sons of God, our identity is in Him, and we have been sent by the Father to serve His purpose on earth, but not to seek for our own recognition and naming.

Therefore, our effectiveness in life and ministry is birthed from the recognition of our identity and purpose in Christ and the passion to pursue it. This is the only path that brings true significance and honour!

Leadership is living and leading by example!

"You call Me the Teacher (Master) and the Lord, and you are right in doing so, for that is what I am. If I then, your Lord and Teacher (Master), have washed your feet, you ought [it is your duty, you are under obligation, you owe it] to wash one another's feet. For I have given you this as an example, so that you should do [in your turn] what I have done to you. I assure you, most solemnly I tell you, A servant is not greater than his master, and no one who is sent is superior to the one who sent him" – John 13:13-16 Amplified Bible.

Jesus demonstrated true honor and strength not by dominating but by serving. This was exemplified as He portrays to His disciples the principle of kingdom ministry, which is service as a servant, as He washes His disciples' feet.

I love the way Bishop Joseph Garlington puts it, "*If you can't pick up the towel, you can't pick up the mantle!*".

Just like the apostle Paul and other godly men recorded in the scriptures, we must be a spiritual pattern (an example of Christ) in our words and actions at all times, so we can provide a godly example for others pointing them to follow Christ, Who is THE Pattern.

We must not allow the wrong mindset of ministry and the pursuit of a godless leadership position robs us of the glory of service. True ministry [that of being a servant of Christ] is our duty. We are under obligation. We owe it. Jesus said, '*blessed and happy and to be envied are you if you know these things and practice them [if you act accordingly and really do them]* - John 13:17.

It is very important for us to set and follow examples that reflect Christ's nature and true kingdom living. Then through the influence of our service we can make a significant impact in our world and in the next generation.

We should adopt the attitude of thinking and constantly asking ourselves the important question; 'what would Jesus do if He is in our position?' This will help us to seek the mind of Christ, through the leading of the Holy Spirit which will guide us into the fulfillment of Christ's desire and will. This is how our lives and works can become more pleasing and acceptable to God.

Leadership is Love!

The ministry of servanthood is by love.

"...having loved His own which were in the world, He loved them unto the end" – (John 13:1).

Love was the motivating factor that led Jesus to serve His disciples by washing their feet. The scripture said, '*He loved them to the last and to the highest degree*'.

It takes love to truly serve someone else without expecting anything in return. The Kingdom of God is a Kingdom of Love, and everything that is done in the name of the Lord must be based on love, because God is love - 1 John 4:8.

There can be no genuine ministry or service without love and humility. Paul the apostle said that, "*love is never proud...*" - 1 Corinthian 13:4-5, therefore love must be humble, which leads us to true ministry serving one another!

"For God is not unrighteous to forget your work and labour of love, which ye have shewed toward His name, in that ye have ministered to the saints, and do minister" – Hebrews 6:10.

Servants serve by love, because service is an expression of love. They desire to minister not for what they get, but what they offer. In the secular realm a boss generally works for the love of what they get. Those with a "boss mentality" will run ministry as a business to profit themselves, but true servants of Christ serve with love and empower others.

Christ's leadership was Compassionate!

"And Jesus, when He came out, saw much people, and was moved with compassion toward them, because they were as sheep not having a shepherd: and He began to teach them many things" – Mark 6:34.

True leaders of the kingdom are compassionate towards the saints and those who are outside the fold. They recognize the needs of others and then act to help. They show warmth love, care and kindness to others. Just like Christ, those who are driven by compassion will teach the truth of Christ and His kingdom and show concern for those suffering.

Not only did Jesus teach the people many things, His compassionate heart caused Him to multiply five loaves of bread and two fishes to feed the hungry crowd of over 5000 people -Mark 6:34-44. He cared about their spiritual life as well as their physical need.

Three times Jesus asked Simon Peter, 'Do You Love Me?' He then said to him, 'Feed My Sheep' - John 21:15-17. Those who are true lovers of God will demonstrate their love by tending the sheep.

Paul the apostle had a deep affection for the church and this became an inescapable pressure of his concern for all the churches. He laboured fervently to reach the Gentiles in far places, driven by this compassion even at the risk of his life.

"But we proved to be gentle among you, as a nursing mother tenderly cares for her own children. Having so fond an affection for you, we were well-pleased to impart to you not only the gospel of God but also our own lives, because you had become very dear to us" – 1 Thessalonians 2:7-8.

"Beside those things that are without, that which cometh upon me daily, the care of all the churches" – 2 Corinthians 11:28.

Chapter Seven

Understanding Core Values and Principles

God is raising a certain quality of people who will be true in all virtue and excellence to His kind of life and leadership.

As followers of Christ and those who are called to spiritual leadership as the servants of Christ, we must reflect the same attributes of Christ. We must be careful that we don't get carried away by the desire for power, prestige and position thus losing the consciousness of Him, Who is the standard.

Leadership is a Privilege and a Responsibility!

Spiritual leadership and ministry is not a right, but a privilege, because no one can take this honor on his own initiative, but only when called to it by God, receiving it of Him.

"And no man takes this honor to himself, but he who is called by God, just as Aaron was" – Hebrews 5:4 NKJV.

More so, there is a 'Double Honour' which is biblically considered as financial benefit given to spiritual leaders, who are faithful to provide effective leadership according to Christ's pattern and principle.

"Let the elders who perform the duties of their office well be considered doubly worthy of honor [and of adequate financial support], especially those who labor faithfully in preaching and teaching. For the Scripture says, You shall not muzzle an ox when it is treading out the grain, and again, the laborer is worthy of his hire" – 1 Timothy 5:17-18 - Amplified Bible.

We are accountable in all things in our service in the name of Christ as ones fulfilling our Master's will. As much as it is a privilege to be counted worthy to be in the service of Christ through His grace, we must also know that it comes with great responsibility.

Its worthwhile studying the parable of the 'Faithful Servant' and the 'Evil Servant' in Luke 12:41-48, because two key principles can be learned from this:

1. A faithful servant knows and does the Master's will - Verse 47.

2. *"...to whomsoever much is given, of him shall much be required - (responsibility)" - Verse 48.*

Great leadership is a product of responsibility. Just as it is said, 'with great power comes great responsibility'.

Leadership is a Call to Humility!

One of the hallmarks of the life and ministry of Jesus is humility and we must have this same attitude and purpose to exemplify His life and ministry.

We cannot speak of the humility of Christ without looking at Philippians 2:5-11. Paul, the apostle, in his letter to the saints in Philippi vividly portrayed to us the very life of Jesus, The Humbled and Exalted Christ, saying:

"Let this same mind be in you which was in Christ Jesus: [Let Him be your example in humility:] Who, although being essentially one with God and in the form of God [possessing the fullness of the attributes which make God God], did not think this equality with God was a thing to be eagerly grasped or retained, But stripped Himself [of all privileges and rightful dignity], so as to assume the guise of a servant, in that He became like men and was born a human being. And after He had appeared in human form,

He abased and humbled Himself [still further] and carried His obedience to the extreme of death, even the death of the cross! Therefore [because He stooped so low] God has highly exalted Him and has freely bestowed on Him the name that is above every name, That in (at) the name of Jesus every knee should (must) bow, in heaven and on earth and under the earth, And every tongue [frankly and openly] confess and acknowledge that Jesus Christ is Lord, to the glory of God the Father".

True humility is meekness, lowliness of mind, absence of self and lack of pride. It is one of the distinct characteristics of the New Man in Christ.

"As holy people whom God has chosen and loved, be sympathetic, kind, humble, gentle, and patient" – Colossians 3:12 GW.

The attitude and character of a servant is humility. It takes humility to serve. If humility is below you, then leadership is above you!

Humility does not reduce your value, but it increases your value and grace in the service of the kingdom of God. In order to live daily by the grace of God, we must be willing to walk in humility.

"Yea, all of you gird yourselves with humility, to serve one another: for God resisteth the proud, but giveth grace to the humble. Humble yourselves therefore under the mighty hand of God, that He may exalt you in due time" – 1 Peter 5:5-6 ASV.

One of the spiritual principles of the kingdom for success and greatness in life is humility. It is a vital key to spiritual elevation which every saint must possess.

"For every one who is exalting himself shall be humbled, and he who is humbling himself shall be exalted." – Luke 18:14b YLT.

The life and character of Jesus was so simplified that even while in the Garden of Gethsemane His accusers could not identify Him or differentiate between Him and His followers, because of His humility. Judas Iscariot had to betray Jesus with a kiss, so they could identify Him.

"And while He was still speaking, behold, Judas, one of the twelve, with a great multitude with swords and clubs, came from the chief priests and elders of the people. <u>Now His betrayer (Judas) had given them a sign, saying, "Whomever I kiss, He is the One; seize Him."</u> Immediately he went up to Jesus and said, "Greetings, Rabbi!" and kissed Him" – Matthew 26:47-49 NKJV.

Today's leaders are easily spotted and known by their exotic robes, expensive toys, bodyguards and entourage. They love to sit in the high place with a special seat and be addressed with titles. They enjoy the praises and reverence of men who prostrate before them and idolize them with these titles. They call it, 'giving honor to the grace, or calling or anointing upon the set-man'. They act like they are holy, humble, loving and caring, yet the saints cannot reach them. They always brag about who they are, what they have done and where they have been etc. People must fill out special forms and go through a third party to book appointments to reach them or pay special fees for their appearance to preach or sing. They call it protocol and 'celebrity status', yet their actions simply display the motive of their hearts as demigods, because they seek position, popularity and fame. They no longer participate with the saints in worship to God, but walk in majestically with pride after praise and worship is over just to hold the microphone and become the center of attraction.

Oh, That God would humble us to know that it is not about us, it is all about Him!

We need to understand the grace and discipline of humility. Dr. Steven C. Riser gave some important views regarding the 'Nature of Humility'. Here is a summary of some of his points:

He said, 'Humility is not primarily an attitude toward oneself but towards God and others'.

1. Humility is an essential characteristic of a truly godly individual. It involves recognizing our total inability to accomplish anything for God apart from His grace (John 15:5).

2. Humility needs to be the habitual attitude of a child of God. A humble person recognizes reality, namely that all we are and have is from God and that we are the object of God's undeserved redeeming love....A genuine spirit of humility is essential to a proper estimate of oneself, one's gifts and one's calling. True humility is not to think too low or too high but to think rightly and truthfully concerning oneself (Rom. 12:3).

3. A humble mind and heart is foundational to all the other graces and virtues. It's an essential prerequisite to experiencing the grace of God.

4. Those that know God will be humble and those that know themselves can't be proud.

Humility is a virtue and a strong foundation that has kept many in life and ministry. Study of 2 Chronicles 32:24-26 and 2 Chronicles 34:24-28 reveals that humility can even avert the wrath of God.

True humility will cause us to remain accessible despite our status and accomplishment, and have a teachable spirit regardless of how much we already know.

"Take My yoke upon you, and learn of Me; for I am meek and lowly in heart: and ye shall find rest unto your souls" - Matthew 11:29.

The instruction of the Lord Jesus Christ is to take His yoke and learn of Him. <u>We are not only instructed to learn *of* Him, but to learn *from* Him.</u>

One thing to learn of Him and from Him is His meekness and lowly heart, [which is His character of gentleness and humility]. The blessedness of this learning brings relief, ease and recreation to our soul, causing us to find rest.

If we follow the patterns and principles from His Word as we look to Him as our example, we will never go wrong.

Leadership is a Call to Integrity!

Integrity is an unimpaired condition of being honest, having strong moral principles and artistic value. It is a quality of life and a state of being upright, complete and undivided.

Leaders must serve with a clear conscience, without duplicity. They must be trustworthy. God delights in people who walk in integrity of heart and live honorably in every way.

Jesus is an example of perfect integrity, and through Him we are able to aim towards true integrity as we serve His purpose in all things. Leadership is an adherence to God's moral values, without compromising His commands and the integrity of His word to twist it to fit our lifestyle because of the revolving world around us.

In this changing and ungodly world we live in today, it is obvious that our integrity is important. The Church is desperately in need of true kingdom leaders with Christ-likeness, who are honest, transparent, God-fearing, purposeful, focused, goal oriented and above all, balanced in the truth. There is no time for superficial leadership. Integrity is essential! It is a life of virtue and excellence that we must fix our minds on – (Philippians 4:8).

Integrity will keep us stayed tenaciously on God as leaders, regardless of any opposition, temptation and challenge the enemy brings - (Psalm 25:21, Psalm 26:1).

Integrity will allow us to faithfully serve and tender the sheep with a pure heart and uprightness - (Psalm 78:72).

Integrity will guide us - (Proverbs 11:3), and integrity will bring blessings upon the children in the house - (Proverbs 20:7).

"*The supreme quality for leadership is unquestionably integrity. Without it, no real success is possible*" - Dwight D. Eisenhower.

Leadership is a Call to Faithfulness!

Faithfulness is loyalty, being dependable and steadfast to whatever we are bound to by pledge, duty or obligation as bond servants of Christ. Faithfulness is a quality of being committed, accurate and true to facts. To be a faithful leader is to be trustworthy and able to be depended upon. One can entrust kingdom responsibilities to our care, knowing that we will be loyal to bear and continue that stewardship.

Most divisions and breakdowns in churches, marriages and business partnerships are caused by lack of loyalty, which ultimately results in lost opportunities.

Jesus Christ is a perfect example of faithfulness. His total reliability and constancy was seen in His personal character, and made known by His words, works and actions. Jesus was faithful to His Father's business, not seeking to do what pleased Himself, but doing only the will of the Father who sent Him - Luke 2:49, John 5:30. He kept on faithfully finishing His work - John 17:4. He did not change.

As leaders, we must demonstrate this same character of Christ and remain faithful in our obedience to keep to our word regardless of whether others do or not.

"Let a man so account of us, as of the ministers of Christ, and stewards of the mysteries of God. <u>Moreover it is</u> <u>required in stewards, that a man be found faithful</u>" - 1 Corinthians 4:1-2.

<u>Leadership is a Call to Submission!</u>

Submission can be broken into two words {Sub-Mission} to give us a better understanding of this call to submission:

"Sub" - meaning to come "under", "below" or "beneath".

"Mission" - an important assignment, purpose or life's work to be carried out.

Submission {"Sub"-"mission"} therefore means to yield oneself to another's will or authority in fulfillment of an important assignment. It is a life of humility and obedience.

Without doubt, Jesus Christ revealed this character of Sub-Mission to us as He took upon Himself the form of a bondservant, in that He became like men. And after He had appeared in human form, He humbled Himself and became obedient to the extreme of death, even the death of the cross to fulfill the will of His Father –(Philippians 2:5-8).

Jesus is a perfect example for us of a surrendered life. He willingly placed His life and desires in full submission to the Father's will.

"He went on a little farther and bowed with His face to the ground, praying, "My Father! If it is possible, let this cup of suffering be taken away from Me. Yet I want Your will to be done, not Mine" - Matthew 26:39 NLT.

"For I came down from heaven, not to do Mine Own will, but the will of Him that sent Me" - John 6:38.

Kingdom leadership is not a call to usurp a position of power and importance, but it is a call of responsibility to yield ourselves to the will and authority of Christ in fulfillment of His purpose and His will, and not our own desires and will.

If we embrace this mindset, then our heart will seek His patterns and principles to do things the way He wants, and in the order that He has set for His Church.

Our only desire should be for God's sovereign rule: "Thy kingdom come. Thy will be done, on earth as it is in heaven" - Matthew 6:10 NIV.

Leadership is a Call to the Word and Prayer!

Another important example we see in the life of Jesus, which every believer in Christ must draw from, is the secret of being alone with the Father. Jesus had a habit of withdrawing Himself constantly from the crowd to be alone with His Father to pray and to seek His will.

"And after He had dismissed the crowds, He went up on the mountain by Himself to pray. When evening came, He was there alone" - Matthew 14:23 ESV.

The effectiveness of Christ's ministry came from His time being alone with the Father. This brought strength and fulfillment to His assignment. The act of seeking the Father's will through prayer and the Word is never a wasted time.

"And it came to pass in those days, that He went out into a mountain to pray, and continued all night in prayer to God. And when it was day, He called unto Him His disciples: and of them He chose twelve, whom also He named apostles" - Luke 6:12-13.

Jesus didn't do anything without first spending time with the Father to seek and know His will, even before appointing and commissioning His apostles. Out of His time being alone with the Father came a demonstration of the glory of God through Him to heal all kinds of sickness, disease and to bring deliverance from demons.

"Then the twelve called the multitude of the disciples unto them, and said, It is not reason that we should leave the word of God, and serve tables......But we [the apostles] will give ourselves continually to prayer, and to the ministry of the word" - Acts 6:2,4.

The apostles learnt this act from being with Jesus and they knew the importance of giving themselves to prayer and to the ministry of the word for the success of their work. They refused to be distracted to serve tables!

The challenge and busyness of service today can often distract and rob us of the joy of intimacy with God, our Father. Religion keeps us busy with service for the Lord and robs us of our service to the Lord, which is the purpose of service. We must set our priority in order!

Being alone with the Father is a place of rest and rejuvenation. It is also the act of waiting upon the Lord.

"But they that wait upon the Lord shall renew their strength; they shall mount up with wings as eagles; they shall run, and not be weary; and they shall walk, and not faint" - Isaiah 40:31.

God is looking for a people who are passionately in love with Him with their whole heart, and who would demonstrate this in their time alone with Him in prayer and abiding in His Word, because He longs for such intimacy. God is seeking for a desperate heart with a deep desire to encounter Him, to be with Him and to be filled with His Spirit.

It is essential that we master the art of being alone with God in His presence to be a conduit of His revelation and life to His Body (The Church).

"*Lord, make me a desperate lover of the secret place to be alone with You so that I may behold Your glory and know Your manifold wisdom*". Let this be your desire and prayer!

Leadership is a Call to Holiness!

To be holy is to be separated unto the Lord. It is a lifestyle of total devotion to God as we are divinely branded for His purpose. It is to be morally pure.

Holiness is the character of God. It is an attribute of God that we must give assent to, to guide and govern our lives. Every leader must bear the mark of holiness unto the Lord in all things. This self-discipline of holiness is a necessity for every believer and for leaders alike in order not to miss the mark of God's purpose for our lives as we pursue His high calling.

"For God saved us and called us to live a holy life. He did this, not because we deserved it, but because that was His plan from before the beginning of time—to show us His grace through Christ Jesus" - 2 Timothy 1:9 NLT.

Chapter Eight

Rediscovering the Message of Jesus

Another important aspect of the Patterns and Principles of Christ is the rediscovering of the original message and mission of Jesus Christ, because this is fundamental to the ultimate purpose of the Church.

Without doubt, the Church will lose her prominence and significance in the community due to misconceptions of the message and mission of Jesus Christ. If we lose the essence of the message of Jesus then we have lost the purpose of our salvation, and have missed the mark of His high calling as a Church.

The aspect of the gospel message of Christ cannot be over-emphasized. The primary gospel message of Jesus Christ is the Kingdom of God. As you go through the scriptures, it clearly reveals that this was the only gospel message Jesus preached and taught according to the New Testament.

"From then on, Jesus began to preach and to say, "Repent, because the kingdom from heaven is near!" - Matthew 4:17 ISV.

"And He (Jesus) said unto them, I must preach the kingdom of God to other cities also: for therefore Am I sent" - Luke 4:43.

"And Jesus went about all Galilee, teaching in their synagogues, and preaching the gospel of the kingdom, and healing all manner of sickness and all manner of disease among the people" - Matthew 4:23.

"And Jesus went about all the cities and villages, teaching in their synagogues, and preaching the gospel of the kingdom, and healing every sickness and every disease among the people" - Matthew 9:35.

"Now after that John was put in prison, Jesus came into Galilee, preaching the gospel of the kingdom of God, And saying, The time is fulfilled, and the kingdom of God is at hand: repent ye, and believe the gospel" - Mark 1:14-15.

"And it came to pass afterward, that He (Jesus) went throughout every city and village, preaching and shewing the glad tidings of the kingdom of God: and the twelve (disciples - apostles) were with Him" - Luke 8:1.

The same gospel message of the Kingdom of God was what Jesus ordained and commissioned His followers to preach. The apostles of Jesus Christ in the New Testament preached nothing but the Kingdom of God, with Jesus Christ being the center of it all.

"He (Paul the apostle) proclaimed the kingdom of God and taught about the Lord Jesus Christ—with all boldness and without hindrance!" - Acts 28:31 NIV.

"But when they believed Philip as he proclaimed the good news of the kingdom of God and the name of Jesus Christ, they were baptized, both men and women" - Acts 8:12 NIV.

If the Kingdom of God was the primary message of Jesus and that of the New Testament Church and apostles, it means this same gospel message of the Kingdom of God is the same message the Church of today must proclaim. Anything less than the gospel of the Kingdom of God is not the message of Jesus Christ.

"And this good news of the kingdom (the Gospel) will be preached throughout the whole world as a testimony to all the nations, and then will come the end" - Matthew 24:14 Amplified Bible.

Every true New Testament Apostolic Church must receive and proclaim the Kingdom of God, as it is the only message that must be preached to all nations, because the Kingdom of God is the principal assignment and function of an apostolic people.

It is worth also noting the central theme of the message of the Kingdom of God, which is "JESUS". The Kingdom is about Kingship. The Lord Jesus Christ is the KING over the Kingdom of God. We must continue to emphasize 'Christ Jesus' in the message. Any message void of Christ and the revelation of His Kingdom is a distraction from God's original purpose, and it does not fulfill His will. If we miss the focus of Jesus in the gospel message of the Kingdom, then we have lost the true essence of the message, and have not preached the gospel of the Kingdom of God. The gospel must be christocentric. Christ should be the center and the only focus of the message.

Whenever the message of the Kingdom is preached it must activate the Christ in us and release us into the reality of our New Creation in Him. Any gospel message and revelation that is preached which obscures this truth of Christ is inaccurate and false, because it obscures God's Self-revelation to us.

It behooves me to say, 'the message of Jesus Christ is not the gospel of escapism or the Law, which is the Mosaic tenets of legalism by works. More so, the gospel of the Kingdom is not healing, deliverance, miracles, prophecy or prosperity. Don't get me wrong! I absolutely believe in the supernatural acts and manifestations of the Holy Spirit as well as prosperity because they play an integral part in the reality and manifestation of the glory of God. However, these concepts are NOT the message itself that Jesus asked His followers to preach, they are the things that accompany the message of the Kingdom when preached.

"Then He (Jesus) called His twelve disciples (apostles) together, and gave them power and authority over all devils, and to cure diseases. And He sent them to preach the kingdom of God, and to heal the sick" - Luke 9:1-2.

"These twelve (apostles) Jesus sent out and commanded them, saying....And as ye go, preach, saying, 'The kingdom of heaven is at hand!' Heal the sick, cleanse the lepers, raise the dead, cast out devils: freely ye have received, freely give" - Matthew 10:5, 7-8.

We must understand clearly the instruction of Jesus to His disciples. He summoned to Him His Twelve disciples and gave them power and authority over unclean spirits (demons) to cast them out, and to heal all kinds of sickness and all kinds of disease. He then sent them out, charging them, saying, 'as you go, preach the Kingdom of God, and heal the sick (healing), cleanse the lepers, raise the dead (miracles), cast out demons (deliverance). Freely you have received, freely give (prosperity).

Jesus never said to them go preach healing, miracles, deliverance or prosperity, He charged them to go preach the Kingdom of God, which is the gospel message, but while they are preaching the Kingdom of God, they are empowered to perform these divine acts of healing, miracles, deliverance, prosperity etc.

This is where the Church has missed the divine commission of Christ to the nations. The challenge we face is the perversion of the true essence and purpose of the gospel of Christ, which is the Kingdom of God. This is because of the dogmatic theology that has been handed over to the Church through the ages, hijacking and diverting the focus and purpose of the saints away from the knowledge of Christ and who we are in Him, and teaching instead human philosophy and the ideology of demons (doctrines of demons).

We have preached the supernatural signs and wonders of God that should follow the message, as the message. But we have not preached the Kingdom of God which is the message of Jesus. Therefore, the Church of today must rediscover the original message of Jesus Christ, which is the Kingdom of God, and return to this ancient truth as we proclaim the reign and rule of God in the earth as it is in the heaven.

The present proclamation of the gospel of healing, miracles, deliverance, prophecy, prosperity and so forth as the primary focus of the message at the expense of Christ, is not the message. 'We cannot continue to preach ONLY on the temporal things and call it the eternal gospel of the kingdom'. We must be very careful not to prostitute the ministry and manipulate the people in ignorance because of miracles, prophecy, fortune and riches.

The message of the kingdom of God is foundational to the building of God's House. Once we lay hold of the revelation of the Kingdom and the concept of it, then we can begin to advance in other areas and fulfill our part in establishing and advancing God's will on earth as it is in heaven.

Let me re-emphasize this again. I absolutely believe in the supernatural acts and manifestations of the Holy Spirit in healing, miracles, deliverance, prophecy and prosperity etc, because God continues to manifest them through our lives and ministry today. They are part of the principles of Christ. What the scripture is saying is that these things or concepts are the supernatural signs that should follow the believers and be a confirmation of the message but, they are not the message, the Kingdom of God is the message.

"But seek (aim at and strive after) first of all His kingdom and His righteousness (His way of doing and being right), and then all these things taken together will be given you besides" - (Matthew 6:33 Amplified Bible).

<u>The Kingdom of God must become our absolute priority and goal in all things, because this is the mission and mandate of God.</u>

Our mindset and understanding must shift to a place of accurate revelation of what the Kingdom of God is not, and what it is, if we are going to fulfill God's purpose on earth.

Firstly, we need to define what the Kingdom of God is!

The Kingdom of God is His Kingship, His Rule, His reign, His authority. The Kingdom of God is a concept in which the will, wish and desire of the King is the same as His laws. The Kingdom of God is righteousness and peace and joy in the Holy Spirit (Romans 14:17) and it reigns in the heart of those who have accepted the Lord Jesus Christ.

We must get back to the preaching and teaching of the Kingdom of God. If Jesus Christ is the standard then we must all flow together in one direction as a unified body proclaiming His message, the Kingdom of God.

Chapter Nine

Revelation: Key to Understanding Spiritual Knowledge

The greatest challenge we have is our ignorance of God's patterns and principles. This has kept us bound in our own ways. The irony of the matter is we are so entrenched in our ignorant ways that we have built systems and regulations which keep us in our ignorance. Therefore, we need a spiritual revelation.

If you don't have a revelation you're going to be stuck in what you know, and what you know is what you've already experienced. New things are birthed from progressive revelation.

You will never learn new things or gain fresh revelation knowledge of Christ and His Kingdom when you think and act as one who knows all things better than others. Therefore, every leader must have a teachable spirit to learn the patterns and principles of Christ and His kingdom.

A revelation is not just the unveiling of the unknown, but it is an appeal to us to something higher and a progressive walk towards the fulfilment of divine purpose and destiny.

Spiritual revelation is a necessity for changing habitual behavior and inaccurate patterns that do not reflect the mind of Christ for His Kingdom, and it comes only by divine encounters through the Holy Spirit as God breaks forth upon us to confront our ways and to reveal His ways to us.

Hearing God or being confronted with a divine encounter will unfold things supernaturally. It does not only bring spiritual knowledge and understanding of things, but it brings a renewal and a change of mind in our set-ways to embrace God's will.

This was the case with Paul the apostle, who was known by his native name; Saul of Tarsus. He fought relentlessly against the Way of God by persecuting the disciples of the Lord. He chased them into foreign lands, beating, imprisoning and causing them to be put to death (Acts 26:11, Galatians 1:13) *though he sincerely thought he was doing the will of God.*

In his testimony, Paul said:

"I myself was convinced that I ought to do many things in opposing the name of Jesus of Nazareth" - (Acts 26:9 ESV).

His absolute conviction resulted to the extreme measure he took to fulfill his duty for God by the havoc he made to the church. Unfortunately, he was fighting against the very God he thought he was helping, simply because he was ignorant of God's way.

As he stood before king Agrippa to recount his conversion (Acts 26:1-19), he said, it took a divine encounter in the form of a heavenly vision, as a bright light shone down from heaven knocking him off his donkey to the ground and then hearing the voice of the Lord speaking to him showing him the way (Acts 9:1-6).

His response afterward was, "*Lord, what do You want me to do?*". He was not disobedient to the heavenly vision (Acts 26:19). I believe this should be the attitude of our heart to receive spiritual knowledge (revelation).

Revelation empowers the saints and awakens within us the freedom we have in Christ.

"As He approached Jerusalem, He saw the city and wept over it [and the spiritual ignorance of its people], saying, "If [only] you had known on this day [of salvation], even you, the things which make for peace [and on which peace depends]! But now they have been hidden from your eyes. For a time [of siege] is coming when your enemies will put up a barricade [with pointed stakes] against you, and surround you [with armies] and hem you in on every side, and they will level you to the ground, you [Jerusalem] and your children within you. They will not leave in you one stone on another, all because you did not[come progressively to] recognize [from observation and personal experience] the time of your visitation [when God was gracious toward you and offered you salvation]." – Luke 19:41-44 Amplified Bible.

As Jesus came to Jerusalem and saw the city, He wept over it because of the spiritual ignorance among the people. They were dull and not able to discern the time of their visitation of the long-awaited Messiah they hoped for. He was right in their midst, yet they did not know Him.

"My people are destroyed for lack of knowledge [of My law, where I reveal My will] Because you [the priestly nation] have rejected knowledge, I will also reject you from being My priest. Since you have forgotten the law of your God, I will also forget your children" – Hosea 4:6 Amplified Bible.

Ignorance disempowers the Church from her divine authority, her sphere of influence and her true purpose on earth. Ignorance will rob us of our identity in Christ and dispossess us of our peace and inheritance.

The fallen state of man and the moral degeneration of the church is because of ignorance, but walking in spiritual knowledge and understanding of Christ and His purpose will bring a reform in all levels. Not only are we transformed, but we experience change in all things.

A revolution is birthed out of a revelation. When we have a clear revelation of God and His patterns and principles; when we position ourselves in Christ, we will become a kingdom revolutionist, able to make a significant impact in our world by bringing a positive and Godly transformation to our communities and the nations.

The Holy Spirit leading:

In this season, some of the theology and traditional concepts form a part of our philosophy and spiritual mindset will need to be redefined more accurately so we can be positioned perfectly in the will of God to fulfill His purpose. This means that we must allow the Holy Spirit to constantly renew our mental attitude and change the way we think.

"Let the Spirit change your way of thinking" - Ephesians 4:23 CEV.

Often, we are preoccupied with our personal agenda and we neglect the will and principles of God. In the pursuit for success and fulfillment of purpose, we must always allow the Holy Spirit to lead us and be in control irrespective of the pressing demands of our flesh with its carnal desires, which may seem right and profitable to us at that time [but these desires won't produce the fruits of righteousness].

God's will (His Kingdom) must always be principal in all our works and ways in order to fulfill the will and purpose of the Father.

The more we learn to listen to the Holy Spirit and the Word of God, the more we will be aligned in our spirit, soul and body to God's purpose and to do His will.

Hearing the Voice of the Spirit:

One of the unique and defining characteristics of the sons of God is the ability to hear the voice of God and be led by the Holy Spirit.

"My sheep hear My voice, and I know them, and they follow Me" - John 10:27.

"For as many as are led by the Spirit of God, they are the sons of God" - Romans 8:14.

We will not be able to follow the patterns and principles of God except there is a clear revelation of His will and His ways to us. This revelation is only given to us when we are inclined to hear and obey what the Lord is saying to us by His Spirit.

If we are spiritually dull to the voice of the Spirit of God speaking to us, we will miss the true purpose of God and fail in our assignment. This is why it is very important to hear God accurately. We must learn to listen to God's voice always; meaning - at all times and in every circumstance, because this is important for the fulfillment of our divine purpose and destiny.

God has given to us the ministry of the prophet, as well as the other five-fold ministry gifts, which carries the grace of Christ to help us hear and obey His voice. All five ministry gifts are vital for the maturing of the saints according to Ephesians 4:4-13. However, it is important that we develop our spiritual ears to hear God personally and directly for ourselves, without the constant dependence on these ministry gifts, because one of the signs of spiritual development and maturity is our ability to hear and obey God for ourselves. [This is one of the main purposes why the prophetic ministry is given - to activate us to hear from God].

Whatever it takes we need to position ourselves to hear God's voice.

How To Hear The Holy Spirit:

You hear the Holy Spirit when you abide in the Word – Focusing on the Word by spending time in the Word and being diligent with it daily.

You hear the Holy Spirit when you pray – Prayer is a two-way dialogue. It is you talking to God and God talking to you. Too often, our prayers are dominated by us talking to God and not listening to Him. We must learn the act of silence in His presence during our prayer time and allow the Lord to speak to us through the Holy Spirit as He reveals things to us and impresses His will in our heart. God is always speaking, but the question is; are we listening?

You hear the Holy Spirit when you listen to God-sent men/women who function by the gifts of the Spirit – The five-fold ministry gifts are given to us by the Lord to be a mouth-piece to the Church. Those who are Spirit-filled and Spirit-led will bring direction of the Holy Spirit to us when we listen to them. They are a prophetic voice bringing prophetic words. You can hear the Holy Spirit through the wise counsel they bring from the Lord.

You hear the Holy Spirit when you develop Fellowship with the Holy Spirit – We must learn to develop friendship and communion with the Holy Spirit, praying always in the Spirit (speaking in tongues). Make it a habit to talk to the Holy Spirit just as you would speak with a friend who is sitting in front of you. The Holy Spirit is a Person, and He delights in your communion with Him.

Tuning in to His Frequency:

It is important to recognize and celebrate the past seasons of God and His dealings with us during the process of the fulfillment of His eternal purpose and promises. But we must be very careful not to continue to celebrate and camp around those seasons, thereby making an idol of them when the Lord has moved on to something better concerning His eternal plan and purpose for us.

Through the scriptures and the journey of the children of Israel, which is recorded for us as a biblical example - we can clearly see and learn from the pattern and principles as revealed through the seasons of Passover, Pentecost and Tabernacles.

There was nothing wrong with Passover and Pentecost, because they were part of the fulfillment of God's purpose. They restored and revealed certain truths which are parts of and foundational to God's eternal purpose, BUT they were not the complete revelation and fulfillment of God's eternal purpose without the full manifestation of Tabernacles. We must understand the purpose and be established in it, and continue to progress beyond to the next. We must move on!

This is the major challenge that we have with the Church today which continues to limit us from reaching forward to what is ahead. We have moved from "Passover" (which is a type of the evangelical season) to "Pentecost" (which is a type of the Pentecostal and charismatic season), but we have camped around these seasons and we refuse to move beyond, [to make the transition to "Tabernacles" (which is a type of the present Kingdom Apostolic Season).

This illustration for today indicates that these seasons were designed by the Holy Spirit until the time of reformation imposed upon them. Reformation brings a new way of thinking and doing things. This we must seek after.

We cannot afford to miss what God is doing in this season. We need to seek the Holy Spirit to guide us and reveal to us the will of Christ. It is REFORMATION time!

Chapter Ten

Perspective on the Apostolic Commission

"And Jesus came and said to them, "All authority in heaven and on earth has been given to me. Go therefore and make disciples of all nations, baptizing them in the name of the Father and of the Son and of the Holy Spirit, teaching them to observe all that I have commanded you. And behold, I am with you always, to the end of the age." - Matthew 28:18-20 ESV.

What we know today as 'The Great Commission' was an apostolic charge that the Lord Jesus gave to the first apostles for the transformation of all nations for His Kingdom. It is considered to be an 'apostolic commissioning' of the corporate Church because it was her 'sending forth' with authority – {Greek word: "apostello", meaning "to send" or "to go forth" - It is an "authoritative sending" or "to order (one) to go to a place appointed}.

The purpose of the mission is to make disciples of all nations who will become obedient to the faith. It is unmistakably an ambassadorial work of the Kingdom to go colonize the nations through the teachings of Christ, which are the very principles of the Kingdom of God.

To colonize is to send people to settle and to govern over a domain. Studying Genesis 1:26-28, it is clear that God's original purpose for man was for him to have dominion over earth. He was sent to colonize the earth by establishing the will of heaven in the Garden of Eden (earth).

Adam lost His dominion. He lost his authority to govern the earth because of His disobedience. He relinquished his colonial powers to satan. Jesus Christ as the last Adam came and striped all authority and power from satan through His death and resurrection, restoring them back to us.

Now, all authority has been given to us by Christ Jesus. The kingdom of satan has been completely destroyed (Colossians 2:14-15) and we have been raised and seated with Christ Jesus in heavenly places (Ephesians

2:6). Now we are co-heirs and partakers with Christ Jesus (Romans 8:17).

We are kingdom diplomats sent by heaven as its representatives on earth. All authority and power of heaven is upon us as ambassadors of Christ and of the Kingdom of God to fulfill the purpose of God by discipling nations.

The apostolic commission is unmistakably the making of discipleship. It is not an option, but a command! Every believer who has been discipled has a role to play for the fulfillment of this commission.

The fulfillment of this grand command requires the re-evaluation of the Church's current mission, so we can rediscover the true act of apostolic discipleship and refocus on the principle that Christ has given to His Church as ambassadors of His Kingdom. Failure to recover this mandate of the Church would be a lost priority of our primary assignment as a Church to the nations.

Making Disciples of all nations:

The making of disciples is the act of raising and establishing people to become followers of Christ by teaching them to be obedient to Christ's commands regarding the principles of the Kingdom of God.

Making disciples of all nations is *far more* than the traditional concept of doing church, bringing people together as members of a local assembly and having services. It is more than going everywhere and preaching in places without a definite purpose of discipleship. Our strategy for ministry, evangelism, church growth and development should be the making of disciples – [Evangelism to raise believers is not enough, we need to raise disciples].

The 'making of believers' is different from 'making disciples'. There is more to just raising people to believe in Jesus as their savior. The challenge we have is that the church is filled with so many believers, but few disciples; yet, the command is to make disciples [and not believers].

Making disciples is a process of spiritual mentoring to teach and develop people into the full and accurate knowledge of Christ. It requires the modelling of Christ to people, so they can be established in Him, and become like Him as they walk in full obedience to Christ's teachings.

There are three key words to consider from Matthew 28:19-20 in making disciples of all nations: Baptism - Teaching - Obedience.

Baptism:

The Greek Word for "baptism" is "baptizo", meaning to make whelmed (that is to fully wet by immersion in water - It means to dip or submerge in water).

The idea of baptizing people as a requirement for membership into 'our institution' or 'our denomination' or 'our church' is unbiblical.

Baptism is the doctrine of our union with Jesus Christ, not our union with a "church" or a denomination or any institution.

We are commanded to only baptize people "into Christ" through His name. It symbolizes the death and burial of our sinful nature and the resurrection of a newness of life in Christ - Galatians 3:27, Romans 6:3-4.

Baptism illustrates a believer's identification with Christ's death, burial and resurrection. Everywhere the gospel is preached and people are drawn to faith in Christ Jesus, they are to be baptized into Christ. Baptism is an essential condition for discipleship. This was why the principle of the early church was first to baptize those who expresses their faith in Christ Jesus as they go through the process of discipleship.

"Those who accepted his message were baptized, and about three thousand were added to their number that day. They devoted themselves to the apostles' teaching and to fellowship, to the breaking of bread and to prayer" - Acts 2:41-42 NIV.

It's important for us to understand the order of things in the early Church as a pattern to follow.

Teaching:

Those who are drawn to the Lord by their faith in Christ Jesus must be taught the sound doctrine of Christ. All discipling should involve teaching. We need to capture the heart of our calling as the Church - to make disciples; and discipling is teaching.

Believers in Christ Jesus must be discipled, by being taught the full and accurate knowledge of the Lord Jesus Christ.

Discipleship requires submission to the process of teaching the command of Christ Jesus.

Obedience:

Walking in obedience to the command of Christ is a prerequisite for discipleship, because it's a demonstration of the commitment of our love for the Lord. By the act of our total obedience to Christ shall all men know that we are His disciples - John 14:15, John 14:23, John 15:10.

The mark of true discipleship in Christ Jesus is obedience to His Word. The character of obedience must be the fruit of our discipleship as it shows our deep commitment to Jesus Christ and a determination to follow and obey Him.

Church Planting - Making Disciples:

First and foremost, "Church" is not a building used for public worship, or a Christian development program, or a denominational institution. This is the mindset and understanding of many people today and it is a wrong biblical understanding of the Church.

The word "Church" comes from the Greek word "*ekklesia*" which is defined as "*an assembly of called-out ones.*" The root meaning of "Church" is not that of a building, but of people. The ekklesia of Christ is not a physical structure, but a people called out from a system as 'Chosen Ones' who are now established upon Christ.

Having said that, Church Planting is NOT the building of a new worship centre or the starting of a new gathering of people where new services are created. It is NOT the setting up of a new institution, organization, denomination or new ministry location with a Christian name attached.

The apostolic concept of Church Planting is basically the formation of Christ in a people and the establishing of the people upon Christ. The idea is a spiritual setting of Christ in a people to reposition them in their divine purpose and destiny as the body of Christ (The Church) - This is what the New Testament apostolic Church Planting was all about - making people disciples of Christ.

Funnily enough, most theological institutions and church growth movements have taught the people the principle of 'Church Development' in lieu of 'Church Planting', and this has messed up our understanding of the true apostolic concept of Church Planting. This is why our church programs and resources have often been centered on building monuments and magnificent structures of mortar and cement (Church Development), rather than on making disciples of all nations, (Church Planting).

As we make the transition from a 'church mindset' to a 'kingdom mindset', there is a need to refocus and return to Christ's original mandate and commission He gave to His disciples (the apostles), and to His Church, which is an apostolic call to go make disciples, not to go assemble a crowd or build monuments of mortar and cement.

"Therefore, as you go, disciple people in all nations" - Matthew 28:19 ISV.

The planting of the Church is an apostolic assignment to make disciples of people in all nations. A people established in Christ, having been taught to walk in full obedience to the purposes of God's Kingdom.

"... greet the Church that is in their house" - Romans 16:5.

Paul the apostle referred to the Church that meets in their house - *not a church building, but a body of believers - a people.*

Also, the epistles of Paul, which are thirteen New Testament books, were letters written to a people known as the Church, *and not to church buildings.*

When someone says his/her calling is an 'apostle', the first question asked is, 'where is your church' or 'where are the churches you have planted?' They want to see a physical structure that is established, because part of the concept of the apostolic calling is to plant churches [which is correct], but the problem is the limited mindset of traditional thinking that church planting is the establishing of structures with mortar and cement [a physical building] or of the physical gathering of people in a location having worship services.

The early apostles did not build any structure of mortar and cement, which they referred to as the church they had planted and established as evidence of their apostolic calling and ministry; neither did they plant or establish any ministry institution or denomination. Their primary mission and assignment was the planting of Christ in people and establishing the people in the purposes of God and His Kingdom. They did this by proclaiming the Kingdom of God and teaching about the Lord Jesus Christ, as they made disciples of Him everywhere. The Lord was with them, working with them and confirming His word by the miraculous signs that followed.

True New Testament Church Planting is not the building of a physical structure, or the establishment of a gathering of people with a ministry named attached to it, but it is the establishment of Christ in a people.

The greatest confirming and authenticating establishment of true New Testament apostolic ministry are people, who are living evidence of the Lord.

"If I be not an apostle unto others, yet doubtless I am to you: for the seal of mine apostleship are ye in the Lord" - 1 Corinthians 9:2.

The fruit of Paul's apostleship in the Lord was not buildings nor assemblies, but people. The fruit of our ministry should be people, who are planted in Christ and established in the true purposes of God and His Kingdom.

"....upon this rock (Christ) I will build My church; and the gates of hell shall not prevail against it" - Matthew 16:18.

When Jesus asked His disciples one of the most important questions saying; "*who do you say that I am?*", Peter replied, "*You are the Christ, the Son of the living God*" - (Matthew 16:13-16). Jesus answered Peter by telling him that His Father in heaven had given Peter this revelation of Christ. And upon this revelation of Christ was what He was going to build His Church on - and the gates of hell will not prevail against or overpower it. (Matthew 16:17-18).

Jesus Christ is the rock - (1 Corinthians 10:4, Acts 4:10-11, 1 Peter 2:4). When Jesus said, "*I will build My Church*", He was not talking about building a material structure, rather He was talking about a people whose headship will be Christ - a people who are established on the rock [the divine knowledge of Christ revealed by the Father].

If our commission and church programs are not fulfilling this basic principle of planting Christ in a people and making them Disciples of Christ and of His Kingdom, then something is wrong. There must be a radical change of mindset, plan and strategy to return to the original commission the Lord gave to His apostles - Making Disciples. This must become our supreme task.

International Training & Resource Center (ITRC)

One of the strategies of WVCOM International in reaching our goal of *"Declaring the Gospel of the Kingdom, Unveiling the Purposes of God and Impacting the Nations"*, is to build and establish an International Training & Resource Centre (ITRC). A multi–purpose facility that will serve as a base for the WVCOM International office, a 500 seat training/conference hall, media studio, Christian library, offices for our international network partners around the nations, and for our Intercessory Network of Prayers for the nations. It will also provide guest homes for our resident leaders and those in the process of leadership training, and as well serve for Community Development & Empowerment Programs to impact the communities through humanitarian services to the less privileged.

The International Training & Resource Centre (ITRC) will offer the opportunity for leadership training, assistance in the five- fold ministry gifts, conferences/seminars and consulting services.

ITRC will become a prototype Antioch Centre to release matured leaders and ministries into the nations. First, a place of identifying emerging leaders for training and development; and for those already in ministry wanting to make a transition from church to Kingdom - a paradigm shift into a new concept of Kingdom lifestyle and transitioning from the old strategy of church system to an innovative concept of the Kingdom. It is a process of change of the old wineskin for the new, by creating an environment for impartation and development to assist leaders and ministries to make full transition into a Kingdom dimension in the present move of God.

ITRC will teach, train, mentor, mature, and activate gifts and ministries. We will impart, develop, motivate and release leaders and the saints to understanding personal calling and identifying their gifts and talents, so they can function in their God ordained ministry in fulfilling the purposes of God.

ITRC will help disciple, deepen and strengthen the relationship of the leaders with God through the impartation of knowledge and experience with biblical principles.

ITRC will function and operate as a resource and networking center, bringing together leaders and ministries around the world of like vision and purpose to see the Kingdom of God established in the earth. Our desire is that from this center there will be an effective networking, church planting and follow up of leaders and the release of the five-fold ministry as a team and company to the nations.

This is the strategy of WVCOM International to fulfill the vision and mandate of God upon our lives, and we are praying and trusting the Father that this will become a reality. We trust the Lord for the finances to build this facility for the Kingdom of God.

The cost is enormous, but the impact is invaluable.

We humbly ask that you prayerfully consider being in partnership with this assignment through your financial support.

Ministry Booking

To Invite The Author To Speak At A Conference,
A local Church or City/Nation, Please Contact Us At:

World Vision Crusade Outreach Ministries
9 Pegasus Road,
Milnerton, Cape Town 7441
South Africa

Tel: +27 (0)21-828-2345
Mobile: +27 (0)82-228-9180
Email: wvcom2001@yahoo.com
Website: www.wvcom-international.org

Other Books By The Author

Apostolic Strategies for Kingdom Reformation – Series 1
Apostolic Strategies for Kingdom Reformation – Series 2
Apostolic Strategies for Kingdom Reformation – Series 3
The Process of Transition
The Way of the Wilderness
Building According to the Divine Pattern
The Wonders of Grace
Knowing God

These books can be ordered by contacting the ministry office or online our website. Other teaching materials, audios and articles can also be seen online our ministry website:

Visit us online

@

www.wvcom-international.org

www.ingramcontent.com/pod-product-compliance
Lightning Source LLC
Chambersburg PA
CBHW071131090426
42736CB00012B/2086